HOW TO LIVE LIFE STRESS FREE

HUZAIFA SURTI

How to Live Life

Stress Free

Huzaifa Surti

Copyright

Author Bio

Huzaifa Surti is a Youtuber, Speaker, Writer blogger, and author of two books

Huzaifa is an influencer with a positive mindset. He believes in the power of positive thinking and writes about inspiring people not to give up on their dreams and become their greatest version.

He writes extensively on success, self-development, productivity, and motivation. his writing is more than just motivational word, it touches the reader's heart and resonates with them

Huzaifa is a voracious reader and prolific writer. He is passionate about living life to the fullest.

you can reach out to Huzaifa at

Gmail - surti.huzaifa@gmail.com

blog - www.positiveacademyhs.com

Twitter - @surtihuzi

Contents

CHAPTER ONE

5 Useful Tips to Convert Stress to Strength

As much as we try to avoid stress, it is slowly creeping in and becoming a regular part of our lives. I am very familiar with this situation as I was an almost fatal victim of it.
Stress can leave us feeling physically, mentally and emotionally drained. We may not be able to get away from stress entirely, but we can learn how to manage it.

Highly stressful situations are fairly common in life, regardless you are living in the city or suburbs, each have their own set of stress to manage. Sometimes you need to reduce your workload to get some relief, but sometimes you can use your stress as leverage to accomplish great things.
Many stressful situations happen in our personal lives and our work. Most problems can be solved. You just have to manage your stress so it doesn't control you by converting stress into something positive with these few useful tips to overcome your stress.

1) Look on the bright side of life.
Studies demonstrate that optimists tend to have a more positive reaction to stressful situations.
While pessimists are busy blaming all possible factors, optimists recognize it as the "get up and go hormone," channelling its power for good.
Remember being an optimist doesn't hurt.

2) Keep your cool.
Very few things in life are real crisis. When you get stressed, it is simple for your blood to begin to boil and you may lose your temper.

In our minds, we tend to make things into a bigger deal than they actually are. You need to deal with your expectations.

In the event that something doesn't work out the way you expect it to be, you shouldn't give that a chance to wreck you.

Keep calm. You can be more successful if you stay calm under pressure.

3) Focus on what you can control.

One of the most positive things you can do when faced with worry or anxiety is to remember what you can control and what you can't.

Unfortunately, many individuals invest energy feeling awful about things they can't change or control.

How about writing out a list of stress and put them into two groups. One group holds the things you can control. The other group is for the things you can't control. Ignore that second group and pick an item to work on in the first. This will start to unravel the anxiety and push you toward your objective.

4) Appreciate what you have.

People love to compare ourselves with others. However, we do as such from a position of shortcoming.

Things can sometimes fall apart, and it is outside your control.

When things seem like they are really bad, you can manage your stress by shifting your focus to being grateful for what you have instead of what you don't.

If you want things to improve you have to focus on what you want, not what you don't want. When consider how privileged you are, you will be you will begin to feel better in a split second.

5) Determine what truly matters.

Although many of us are helpful and would gladly lend a helping hand to friends or clients, we still need to set limits with them.

It is easy to get sucked in with their problems and allow it to stress you out too. Remember that stress can leave us feeling physically, mentally and emotionally drained. By setting up certain boundaries, it would enable you to remove the feeling of obligation and making someone else's problem your stress. Keep in mind that everything in life is not an emergency. In high-stress situations, you may need to step back and evaluate whether this is something that is worth getting so upset over. Ask yourself, "Will this matter to me in a year from now?"

CHAPTER TWO

26 tips for managing stress

1. always take time for yourself, at least 30 minutes per day

2. be aware of your own stress meter, know when to step back and cool down

3. concentrate on controlling your own situation, without controlling everybody else

4. daily exercise will burn off the stress chemicals

5. eat lots of fresh fruit, veggies, bread and water, give your body the best for it to perform at its best

6. forgive others, don't hold grudges and be tolerant no everyone is as capable as you

7. gain perspective on things, how important is the issue?

8. hugs kisses and laughter, have fun and don't be afraid to share your feelings with others

9. identify stressors and plan to deal with them better next time.

10. judge your own performance realistically; don't set goals out of your own reach

11. keep a positive attitude, your outlook will influence outcomes and the way others treat you

12. limit alcohol, drugs and other stimulants, they affect your perception and behaviour

13. manage money well seek advice and save at least 10 percent of what you earn

14. no is a work you need to learn to use without feeling guilty

15. outdoor activities by yourself, or with friends and family can be great way to relax

16. play your favourite music rather than watching television

17. quit smoking it is stressing your body daily, not to mention killing you too

18. nurture your relationship and enjoy them learn to listen more and talk less

19. sleep well with a firm mattress and a supportive pillow don't overheat yourself and allow plenty of ventilation

20. treat yourself once a week with a massage, dinner out, movies moderation is the key

21. understand things from the other persons point of view

22. verify information from the source before exploding

23. worry less it really does not get things completed better or quicker

24. express make a regular retreat to your favourite space, make holidays part of your yearly plan and budget

25. yearly goal setting plan what you want to achieve based on your priorities in your career, relationship etc.

26. zest for life: each day is a gift smile and be thankful that you are a part of the bigger picture.

CHAPTER THREE

Do Give Yourself Permission to Quit When Necessary

Mentally strong people do not give up after their first failure. They know that quitting doesn't make them a loser, and that it takes an even larger amount of mental strength to walk away from a goal.

But they do know when to walk away, especially when their goals have changed (perhaps they had found a better goal) or when they have unknowingly dug themselves into a hole (when things don't go well and they need to walk away before it get worse), for instance.

Mentally Strong People Do Give Themselves Permission to Quit When Necessary

You must never make a rash decision to quit your goals and give up due to frustration, fatigue or disappointment. It is a decision that you need to take seriously, carefully balancing your logical and emotional mind. Spend some time to ponder the advantages and disadvantages of persevering on versus quitting.

My humble opinion is that, just remember **quitting doesn't mean that you are failure**, especially when the reward is not worth it anymore or when the process of achieving your goal don't align with your values and principles. In fact, the smart people knows when to quit instead of blind perseverance. Giving up on one goal could actually be a stepping stone to another goal for your future success.

5 ways to love yourself and your uniqueness

Love. That one word can cause an array of thoughts and mixed feelings. Loving yourself can be not as easy as it sounds, especially as an adolescent or young adult when you are still struggling with your own identity.

Social media, advertising and expectations from society are the main factors for both men and women to struggle with loving themselves.

Instead of constantly judging and shaming others, while making comparisons to celebrities or models, we should celebrate the fact that we do not all look the same, and we should love and accept our flaws because they make us who we are.

Here are some 5 ways to love yourself and your uniqueness:

1) Start your day by loving yourself!

Look into a mirror and tell yourself something loving. "You have the most beautiful smile!"

If you don't feel like doing that then try telling yourself something positive. "You're a very creative and sweet!"

Say anything that makes you feel great and makes you smile! :)

2) Learn to love the skin you are in.

Nourishing your body with healthy food and a sensible diet to keep up your metabolism is a way to honour yourself.

Give yourself some good pampering, like rewarding yourself in a long warm bath soak or a massage or a spa treatment.

Find ways to enjoy, like and love your body. It's the only one you get.

3) It's okay not be perfect.

I'll let you in on a secret: you're not perfect.

But guess what? No one else is perfect either. *Nobody is perfect, even celebrities aren't perfect.*

We all have flaws and that is perfectly okay!

You shouldn't expect yourself to be perfect always because frankly, it is simply impossible.

4) Be Your own cheerleader.
Celebrate all of your accomplishments, no matter how big or small they are.
Be proud of yourself. Be the first to congratulate yourself then let others do it if they want, not the other way around.
It is alright to praise yourself.

5) Be thankful.
At the end of the day as well as all day long, be grateful for all that you have.
Showing gratitude is the quickest way to turn things around.
It will also open the doors for more wonderful things to enter your life.

CHAPTER FOUR

3 Lies You May Be Telling Yourself

Lying is almost always not a good thing. A little white lie can be okay if it is not to hurt someone, but it also depends on the context of it.

However, you cannot deny that too many lies can be chaotic, especially if one white lie leads to a next white lie and to the next, eventually you end up deceiving yourself and the ones you love. Lying to yourself is not very healthy, even though sometimes it treads dangerously on giving yourself a pep talk.

I admit that I do lie to get away from things or just not to hurt the people I know. I told a lot of white lies and some absurd ones too, but I keep myself honest to offset for those lies I told and I don't want to become a compulsive liar like some people I know who will believe in their own lies even though it's obvious that they got caught lying.

What I am about to share may or may not relate to you, but these are the 3 common lies I find a lot of people are telling themselves, including me....

1) I'm Okay.

I want to be okay even though deep down I know I might not.

When I am down or something drastic happens in my life, I always tell myself and to others that 'I'm Okay' even though I am not.

When I was recovering from stroke and coming to terms of the "not normal life" I would be facing, I was treading on the slippery edge of depression.

I learned from that experience that **it's okay to not be okay.**

Telling that myself that I am fine and keeping everything to myself is unhealthy, and in fact that was the tipping point to near depression. I was like in the shadows keeping to myself.

When I started to **reach out for help** and confide in 'stronger' people who are in the light, and they extended their helping hand of encouragements, that's when I started to step out from the shadows and into the light.
Finding an outlet to share what you're feeling helps. That was **Effective Way #7 Write**, I usually write when I am feeling not okay or tell it to my husband or a trusted friend so we can talk about it. After that sharing session, I will feel a sense of good relief.

Admitting that you're not okay can be scary to some but it's better to admit it than to lie to yourself and keep those negative emotions piling up within you.

2) I'm Not Ready To...

Truth is, no one is ever ready for anything, because life is like that. **Expect the unexpected.**

Yes, I am not ready for anything. I told myself ones before I started studying part time while working that I am not ready for the real commitment of time and money away while I just started enjoying the luxurious full pay of professional yet. I told myself that I am not ready to leave my previous corporate life as an engineer with a decent pay, to take things easy, start anew and work from home without a stable monthly pay, but I had to do it ultimately as the stress is killing me as a corporate slave and I could not risk a second stroke.

It's a big change for me, but my husband, my number one fan, was always there to encourage me to step out of my comfort zone, to put health first, and take life by the horns as it comes.
Even If I fall, I should just stand tall and not make the mistake again.

If you say you aren't ready for something, chances are that you either are not all that interested or you are too deep procrastinating - most likely out of fear. However, all you have to do is believe in yourself, **(effective way #4)**

have faith, and take it one step at a time, putting each foot forward, slowly, steadily, surely.

Keep an open mind to your options. Be courageous and take the leap of faith.

3) I Can Do That Tomorrow.

Yes, this an old habit that even I need to break. I have a very bad habit of procrastinating. Always putting things off thinking that I can do it tomorrow, or I can finish it tomorrow.

It was a bad habit during my days of a student, pushing back datelines, giving me sleepless nights.

Old habits die hard, but you don't let the bad habit of procrastinating stop you to finish on what you can finish today, but of course without stressing yourself up over it.

So these are the lies I keep telling myself and I believe some of you may face the same thing. Although lying is in the human nature, we can still help ourselves to improve and refrain from lying that would eventually come back and bite us.

By becoming aware of what you are telling yourself, you can do this by listening to your inner self and tuned into your feelings.

As soon as you feel badly, ask yourself what you are telling yourself that is making you feel badly.

Ask yourself if you are certain that what you are telling yourself is true?

Chances are that you will recognize your pain is caused by the made-up lie.

Next ask yourself what is the truth?

When you have a genuinely strong desire to know the truth, the answer will come through you from your inner and wiser self.

Bring the truth to the wounded part of yourself, and take action based on the truth.

In time to come, your inner dialogue will slowly shift from lies to truth. And truth frees you from the painful feelings that result from the lies.

Be more honest to yourself. A little honesty can go a long way.

The best way to start now is by observing your thoughts. Where are your thoughts running?
thoughts running?
What is your inner voice whispering?

• 12 •

CHAPTER FIVE

Self-care strategies you can do in 10 days

make sleep a Priority

nothing affects our ability to process and handle challenging situations more than adequate sleep when we are well rested, we are better equipped to keep your emotions in check BE productive and find Creative Solutions unfortunately or busy schedule of an keep a good night rest at a day

today take the time to develop night time routine and that is the habit of making Sleep priority

Drink more water

Our society has a habit teaching for diet soda over bottled Water and this isn't good soda coffee and energy drink can be full of sugar and are often more dehydrating they are hydrating

water is an essential ingredient for our body to function properly and without it we feel both physical and mental effects

today drink more water if you have a hard time drinking plain water try adding some lemon and mint for refreshing and detoxifying face lift

Move more

Everyone agrees that exercise is good for you it elevates your mood decrease test and gives you more energy So if we can all agree we should exercise more why are at me letter of time is equal the response well the good leadership and realise the benefits with as retailer standing with a day only, we can find 10 minutes like

today go for walk 5–10-minute exercise on YouTube does some sketching at your dad whatever you too used to move more today than you did yesterday

Spend time with friend

a solid social network makes us happier and there isn't a better way to take care of ourselves then to spend time without friends they hold our hand when we are sad supporters when we are scared and make us laugh in dark time don't wait until next crisis spend time with people who matter

today schedule date for coffee or lunch with the close friend because it is a right thing to do

read a book

reading keeps our mind sharp and active mind better equal to handle stress and life challenges be on a constant veston.in calendar. It will contribute to more positive thoughts and a better outlook on life

today pick book you have always wanted to read and read a page or 10

enjoy your hobby

having time to do something just for fun of it is the ultimate example of self-care everybody feels good when they are doing something they love it is about realising the stress and Chaos of our day in activity we enjoyed

today try something you always wanted to do something you love just for the fun it

take a photo photograph

capture memories and memories remind us of important moments when you take the time to take pictures of our day it gives a chance to slow down and appreciate our surroundings

today take a photo of the things that make you smile

Seek Serenity

find it charges our natural energy and natural energy is what professor power De in which software we can that go around us and focus on your body between them it will be worst feeling more sandal and more economics\

today take 5 minutes. Place and let your mind wander as you focus on your breath

spoil yourself

calling ourselves is not self-indulgence it is necessary important when we take the time to rewind our self that we are special and deserving of good in our lives when we treat ourselves well and when we believe on date more opportunities of abundance will begin to appear

today do something special just for you because you do it

practice gratitude

a big part of self-care is being grateful for all the good in our life when we take the time to practice gratitude, we are changing our mind set an hour window of the world

today take the time to honour themes you are grateful for in your life journal photography and spend time in somewhere drinking attention to it doing this might be the best self-care strategy of all

CHAPTER SIX

How to Live Life Stress Free

Why are we living stress free life? Stress is the major cause of diseases as per the survey, how one can live stress free life?

When you are in nature, such as water, greenery, mountains, we feel so good and we instantly become stress free.

let me tell you story, few weeks before there were some marks on my car, so I went to the mechanic and he told me that it is running in an emergency mode, I asked why it is in an emergency mode? the mechanic told that because of some damage it is working but utilizing more energy with more power consumption, so try to fix this as soon as possible otherwise this car will be damage.

I thought of myself that when people go in emergency mode, when they remain under stressful condition such that the body parts start damaging.

Why people are under stress all the time? we know that 95% diseases which happens is due to stress (Psychologist Say)

Stress is very harmful for our life and health, so we need to get rid of that.

why this stress happens? because we want to achieve those goals which are not in our control and also not in our luck so we become stressful.

you know that lot of things are automatic. In survey from American University, they said that you don't have 80% of life in your hands, you only have 20% of life which you can decide and think.

If 80% life is not in our control then why we are in 80% stressful condition? if you need to come in stress then take the stress for the things which is under your control that is 20%

80% is not in your control and if you don't believe this then let's take a challenge and try to stop the breathing which is automatic for 3 minutes or more by closing your nose, I am sure that you won't be able to do that after 1 minute only the body organs will force you to take breathe.

Meditation is the practice of observing breath

It means breathing is not in our control, we breathe in order to live life. To Breathe properly is to live properly.

Why we come in stressful condition, though lot of functions are automatically happening in our body?

Take Example of your body,

Our Human Body an Amazing Creation

1. your brain processes 400 billion bits of information in second, so much strong and powerful it is. Did you make it? Do we make run?

we just have 2000 bits of information we are aware more than we don't know

2. have you ever think of your heart? 2-gallon blood is pumped into our organs in one second- and 100-gallon blood is pumped by heart into the vessels in one minute.

3. our heart beats 3 billion time in an average life span, you tell me which electricity do you have which you have attached and its working?

without any electricity, it is nature through which your heart is working, 3 billion times your blood is pumped into your vessels

4. do you know the length of your vessels? they are 60000 miles long.

our body is having 100 trillion cells and out of them 10 million cells are dead in one second and in one second 10 million new cells are made.

After sometime our whole body takes new shape, are you doing all this? do you know in your cell in one second 10000 chemical changes happen. do you do this?

if we are not doing this and it is not in our control then why we are in stress?

your life is 80% in control of nature, so please let go of your all troubles and forget them. all happening is good, end this stressful living because when we end stress, we have destroyed 95% diseases and we can live life to the fullest.

See in this Water, Greenery and Mountains doesn't cost you anything and I am not spending anything but if we spend 15 minutes in nature then surely, we can get rid of stress

I wish you have amazing stress-free life, live life well and we can do it

Good Bye

CHAPTER SEVEN

How to Overcome Depression and Anxiety

Mental health is one of the common problems which people are facing nowadays and depression is one of them.

How to Overcome Depression and Anxiety

Depression is a mental state it can be cured

How to Overcome Depression and Anxiety I will try to give simple solutions to these problems

Depression is Suppression - you suffer from depression because you suppress your emotions and don't allow to pass them through you

Meditation - there are different types of meditation which one can practice to get rid of depression, meditation is basically focussing on your breathing. Mindfulness meditation is the one in which you focus on total body awareness, knowing thyself

Spend time in Nature - Nature heals everything, spend some time in nature go out for a walk in the garden barefoot. you will be relaxed and feel great

Listen to Music - Music plays an important role in one's life especially if someone is feeling down it helps us to elevate our mood and raise frequency and vibrations. listen to music which you love.

Watching Funny Videos - Fun is an important part of our life without fun life is nothing, watch funny videos on YouTube or spend time with grandparents and with a kid who is below the age of 10. you will be feeling amazing.

Become Social - in the beginning, you won't be comfortable being social and that's ok but you need to be in talking to the people it may be stranger, family member or a loved one because when you talk to someone you share what you carry which in turn can make you depressed.

Avoid Staying Alone - This is similar to the above but even if you don't have any person with whom you can talk try to go out for shopping or public places which might be of interests to you. this is important because staying alone will lead you to become more depressed.

Make Yourself Busy - When you have a busy schedule doing the work you love, you don't do overthinking and getting involved in the stuff which doesn't bother you much. so, keep yourself busy throughout the day and stay away from negativity.

Avoid Negativity - We are often surrounded by the people which always keeps us in negative mode. you can't do this, this is not of your type, etc.

you are the sum of the people to whom you surround yourself with

so, stay away from such people and in that way, you can get rid of depression.

Eat the right food - You are what you Eat

Eating the right food plays a very important role when you suffer from depression you are actually lacking chemicals in brains such as Dopamine and Serotonin, so in order to get rid of the condition, you need to include foods which are rich in Serotonin-like Banana, Nuts, Eggs, Spinach, etc.

Exercise Every day - Study shows that exercising every day helps you to release endorphins and it reduces depression of about 70%. your mood which changes and you will feel good when you exercise at least 30 minutes per day do your favourite activity like jogging, cycling, running, etc. you can also get involved in sports.

Help Someone Needy - When you help someone you will feel happy automatically, Happiness comes from sharing, so next time when you feeling down or sad, help someone who is seeking help and, in that way, you are helping yourself too.

Reading Books - When you feel alone or down and don't have someone to spend time with, books can be one of your best friends, it improves brain health and you can always learn something from them, reading is a very powerful tool for personal development and sharpening your skills.

Believe in Yourself - When you Believe in yourself you are halfway done - yes, we need to believe in ourselves and must have a never to give up attitude. even if things are not in our favour just trust the process and universe will help you to reach your goal.

Start Counselling - If you are not comfortable sharing with your family or friends you can do the same with the stranger, by seeking a counsellor they will help you to get rid of unwanted thoughts and be positive in life.

Don't Go for Drugs - When you go for drugs you are actually taking a chemical into your body which will definitely cause you harm, anti-depressant has a lot of side effects, so stay away from drugs. remember drugs cannot remove depression but you yourself have the power to overcome it.

Watch Your thoughts Journal Them - Thoughts are very important, thoughts become things. so, whenever some negative thought comes to your mind just journal them all and throw away the paper you will automatically feel good

Use Positive Affirmations - Affirmation is very helpful, affirmation is the statement which you speak into the present tense, words have power when you speak something repeatedly your brain will believe what you speak and it will be manifested in your life.

Be Grateful for What You Have - Gratitude plays a very important role in one's life, if someone is grateful for what he has, he will attract more into his life. so be grateful for what you have and you will be happy.

Learn Something New - When you get involved in learning something new, you tend to forget the state in which your life is, so learn something new it can be a new language, driving a car, traveling to an unknown place, making new friends, etc.

Limit the Use of Social Media - When someone posts something on social media we generally feel negative, felling such as envy, jealousy, hatred comes because we see other more successful, happy and prosperous, we compare ourselves with others. which will lead to more depression.

Monitor Your Self-Talk - When you are alone what self-talk you have with yourself, I am not enough, all is not well, what will happen to me? these are all negative self-talk. so, monitor them and try to make them positive by replacing them with positive affirmations in that way you can get rid of depression.